FAN CLUB

I Love TAYLOR SWIFT

Kat Miller

WINDMILL
BOOKS

New York

Published in 2011 by Windmill Books, LLC
303 Park Avenue South, Suite # 1280, New York, NY 10010-3657

CREDITS:
Editor: Jennifer Way
Book Design: Erica Clendening and Greg Tucker
Photo Research: Ashley Burrell

Photo Credits: Cover, p. 22 Kevin Winter/Getty Images; pp. 4–5, 18, 21 Frank
Micelotta/Getty Images; p. 6 Kevin Winter/ACMA/Getty Images; p. 7 © www.
iStockphoto.com/arpajit arnontavilas; pp. 8–9 Ethan Miller/Getty Images; p. 10
Rick Diamond/Getty Images; pp. 11, 13, 19, 20 Shutterstock.com; p. 15 Austin
K. Smith/Getty Images; p. 16 Dan MacMedan/WireImage/Getty Images; p. 12
Rahav Segev/WireImage/Getty Images; p. 17 Cliff Lipson/CBS/Getty Images.

Library of Congress Cataloging-in-Publication Data

Miller, Kat.
  I love Taylor Swift / by Kat Miller.
     p. cm. — (Fan club)
  Includes index.
  ISBN 978-1-61533-051-5 (library binding) — ISBN 978-1-61533-052-2 (pbk.) —
ISBN 978-1-61533-053-9 (6-pack)
  1. Swift, Taylor, 1989– —Juvenile literature. 2. Women country musicians—
United States—Biography—Juvenile literature. 3. Singers—United States—
Biography—Juvenile literature. I. Title.
  ML3930.S989M55 2011
  782.421642092—dc22
  [B]

                              2010006827

Manufactured in the United States of America

For more great fiction and nonfiction, go to windmillbooks.com.

CPSIA Compliance Information: Batch #S10W: For further information contact Windmill Books, New York, New York at 1-866-478-0556.

Contents

Taylor Swift is one of today's biggest stars. She has **millions** of fans. Many of these fans are kids who look up to Taylor. They love her songs and are always happy to hear her sing.

Taylor's songs come from her heart. One reason for this is that she writes most of

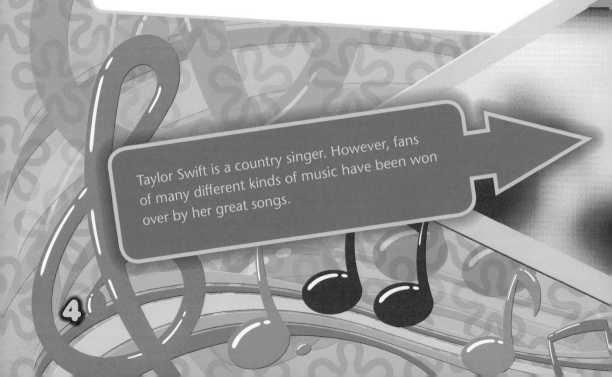

Taylor Swift is a country singer. However, fans of many different kinds of music have been won over by her great songs.

the songs she sings. Many of the songs she writes are based on things that really happened to her. Taylor is a very **talented** songwriter.

Taylor Swift was born on December 13, 1989. Her full name is Taylor Alison Swift. Taylor's parents are Andrea and Scott Swift.

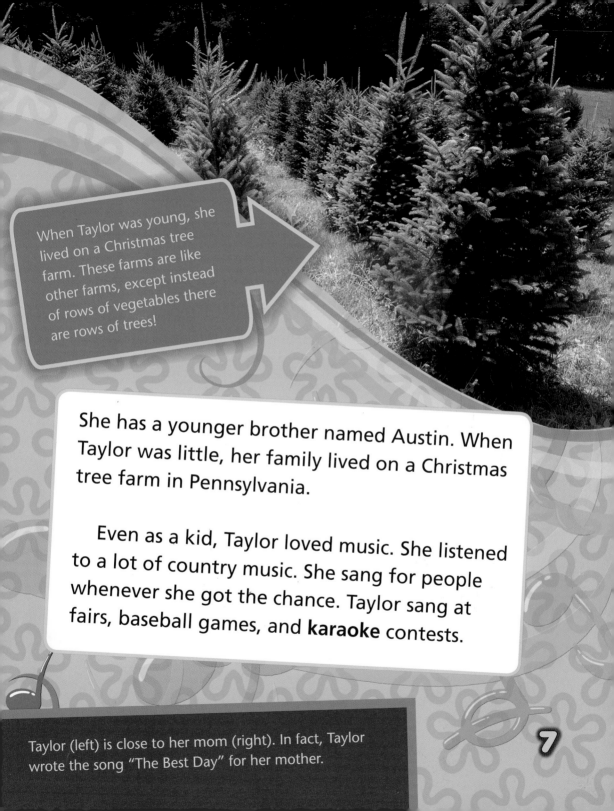

When Taylor was young, she lived on a Christmas tree farm. These farms are like other farms, except instead of rows of vegetables there are rows of trees!

She has a younger brother named Austin. When Taylor was little, her family lived on a Christmas tree farm in Pennsylvania.

Even as a kid, Taylor loved music. She listened to a lot of country music. She sang for people whenever she got the chance. Taylor sang at fairs, baseball games, and **karaoke** contests.

Taylor (left) is close to her mom (right). In fact, Taylor wrote the song "The Best Day" for her mother.

7

A Talented Songwriter

When Taylor was 11, she visited Nashville, Tennessee. This is the city where most country music is made. Taylor dropped off tapes of herself singing to every music company there. Nobody was interested, but she did not give up.

At the age of 12, she started playing the guitar and writing her own songs. When

Taylor often plays along on the guitar while she is singing or writing songs. Today, Taylor plays a guitar made of koa wood.

Taylor was in the ninth grade, her family moved to Hendersonville, Tennessee. This town is near Nashville. There, she started working with other songwriters.

When Taylor was 15, a music **executive** heard her singing at Nashville's Bluebird Café. He offered her a spot on his music **label**. She set to work **recording** songs.

Here, Taylor Swift is singing the song "Our Song," at the 2007 Country Music Association Awards. The song is on the album *Taylor Swift*.

This is the country music singer Tim McGraw. One of Taylor's first hit songs was about hoping that one of McGraw's songs made a boy think of her.

In October 2006, Taylor came out with her first **album**. It was called *Taylor Swift*. The album was a hit. It has Taylor's song "Tim McGraw" on it. In the song, Taylor hopes that a song by Tim McGraw will make a boy she dated think of her.

Taylor's first album won her many fans. Lots of people bought the album. The songs got played a lot on the radio. Next, Taylor toured with other singers. She played shows in many cities and towns. This gave her fans a chance to hear her sing in person.

Nashville, shown here, is said to be the home of country music. Taylor Swift lives in a town near Nashville so that she can be where the music she loves is made.

Taylor also won praise for her songwriting on her first album. In 2007, she won the Nashville Songwriters Association International's songwriter-artist of the year **award**.

Here is Taylor in 2009 performing on the *Today* show.

Fearless Taylor

In 2008, Taylor put out her second album, *Fearless*. Taylor explained the album's name, saying that "fearless is having a lot of fears, but you jump anyway." Many of the songs on the album became hits, such as "Fifteen," "White Horse," "Breathe," and "You Belong With Me."

Here, Taylor is singing on her Fearless Tour. On the tour, Taylor got to wear lots of beautiful dresses, such as this one.

After the album came out, Taylor went on the Fearless Tour. It was her first time headlining, or being the main singer, on a tour.

A Music Superstar

Fearless was a huge hit. It sold more than 5 million copies! In 2009, it sold more copies than any other album in the United States.

Taylor won a total of 4 Grammy Awards in 2010.

16

Taylor was filled with joy when *Fearless* won the Best Country Album at the Grammy Awards in January 2010.

The album won Taylor awards, too. In 2009, she won four American Music Awards. She also became the youngest person ever to be named the **Entertainer** of the Year by the Country Music Association. In 2010, Taylor won four Grammy Awards for *Fearless*, including album of the year.

Taylor and Her Fans

Though she is now a superstar, Taylor still values her fans. She happily signs autographs. Once, she signed **autographs** for nearly eight hours!

Taylor takes time to greet fans and sign autographs whenever she goes to an event.

As someone who is a big music fan herself, she understands how important her music is to her fans. It makes her happy to write songs that other people can enjoy. Taylor has said, "I like to listen to music that's about life. That's what I think my fans like, too."

Here, Taylor Swift talks to fans and signs autographs at the 2009 Country Music Television Music Awards in Nashville, Tennessee.

What's Next for Taylor?

Taylor has a busy life. She acted in the movie *Valentine's Day*, which came out in February, 2010. She also has appeared on several television shows.

Taylor is also working on her third album. She spends lots of time writing songs. Over the years, Taylor has written

Taylor's Fearless Tour has allowed her to play concerts for cheering fans all over the world.

Taylor's fans love to see her sing. Hopefully, they will be able to go to her shows for years and years.

hundreds of songs. She has said that she can't stop writing songs and that songwriting is like breathing to her. Her songs will delight fans for years to come.

Just Like Me!

1 There are many singers whose songs Taylor loves. The singer she says she has learned the most from is Shania Twain.

2 Taylor likes shopping for clothes. Dresses and cowboy boots are some of her favorite things to wear.

3 Tyler likes to watch movies. One of her favorite movies is *Love Actually*.

4 When she was in fourth grade, Taylor won a poetry contest. The poem she wrote was called "Monster in My Closet."

5 Taylor's favorite food is cheesecake.

Glossary

album (AL-bum) A recording or group of songs.

autographs (AH-toh-grafs) Copies of a person's name, written by that person.

award (uh-WORD) A special honor given to someone.

entertainer (en-ter-TAYN-er) Someone who does something that pleases and interests others.

executive (eg-ZEK-yoo-tiv) The head of something.

karaoke (ker-ee-OH-kee) Singing a well-known song for others for fun.

label (LAY-bul) A company that puts out music made by several different artists.

millions (MIL-yunz) One thousand thousands.

recording (ree-CORD-ing) Making a copy of a song so that others can listen to it.

talented (TA-len-ted) Very good at something.

Index

Read More

Rawson, Katherine. *Taylor Swift*. Kid Stars! New York: PowerKids
Press, 2009.

Reusser, Kayleen. *Taylor Swift*. Blue Banner Biographies. Hockessin,
DE: Mitchell Lane Publishers, Inc. 2008.

Tieck, Sarah. *Taylor Swift: Country Music Star*. Big Buddy Biographies,
Set 3. Edina, MN: Abdo Publishing Company, 2009.

Web Sites

For Web resources related to the subject of this book,
go to: www.windmillbooks.com/weblinks and select
this book's title.